Nursery Rhymes Your Mother Never Taught You

Marilyn Huntman Giese

Copyright © 2019 by Marilyn Huntman Giese.

Library of Congress Control Number:	2019915930
ISBN: Hardcover	978-1-7960-6478-0
Softcover	978-1-7960-6477-3
eBook	978-1-7960-6476-6

All rights reserved. No part of this book may be reproduced or transmitted in any form or by any means, electronic or mechanical, including photocopying, recording, or by any information storage and retrieval system, without permission in writing from the copyright owner.

Scripture quotations marked NASB are taken from the New American Standard Bible®, Copyright © 1960, 1962, 1963, 1968, 1971, 1972, 1973, 1975, 1977, 1995 by The Lockman Foundation. Used by permission.

Scripture quotations marked AAT are taken from The Holy Bible: An American Translation. Front Cover. William Frederick Beck. Leader Publishing Company, 1976

Any people depicted in stock imagery provided by Getty Images are models, and such images are being used for illustrative purposes only. Certain stock imagery © Getty Images.

Print information available on the last page.

Rev. date: 11/07/2019

To order additional copies of this book, contact:
Xlibris
1-888-795-4274
www.Xlibris.com
Orders@Xlibris.com
799249

Dedicated to my husband Dr. Stan Giese and our five children: Deborah Ann, Terry Ellen, Dr. Todd Stanley, Jean Frederica, and Pamela Sue.

Contents

Introduction VII

PART 1 — NURSERY RHYMES YOUR MOTHER NEVER TAUGHT YOU—THE PARODIES

Food 3
    Jack Sprat 5
    Little Ms. Muffet 7
    Rub-A-Dub-Dub 9
    Peter, Peter 11
    Little Boy Blue 13

Reading Between The Lines—Food 15

Fun 19
    Mary Had A Little Car 21
    Pussy Cat, Pussy Cat 23
    Jack And Jill 27
    Hickory Dickory Dock 29
    Little Mama Beau-Peep 31
    Mary, Mary, Quite Contrary 33

Reading Between The Lines—Fun 35

People 39
    There Was An Old Woman 41
    Georgie Porgy 43
    Three Blind Mice 45

    Baa, Baa, Black Sheep 47
    A Diller, A Dollar 49
    Little Jack Horner 51

Reading Between The Lines—People 53

Politics 57
    All Around 59
    Old (Nat) King Cole 61
    Humpty Dumpty 63
    Hey Diddle Diddle 65
    Simple Simon 67
    The North Wind Doth Blow 69
    Who Killed Cock Robin? 71

Reading Between The Lines—Politics 73

PART II — TRADITIONAL NURSERY RHYMES MY MOTHER TAUGHT ME 77

About The History Of Traditional Nursery Rhymes 79
About Traditional Nursery Rhymes Today 81
Traditional Nursery Rhymes 83
    Food 85
    Fun 87
    People 89
    Politics 91

Acknowledgments And After Thoughts 95
Selected References 97

Introduction

Part I: Nursery Rhymes Your Mother Never Taught You—The Parodies

Part I of Nursery Rhymes Your Mother Never Taught You is a collection of twenty-four parodies meant to brighten your day and tickle your funny bone. They lift the meaning of rhymes you learned as a child to new heights of absurdity. Each revision came into being as a reaction to the politics and people of the 21st Century. There are four sections: Food, Fun, People, and Politics. At the end of each section under the title Reading Between the Lines there are three suggestions per parody for thoughts to ponder. They are good conversation starters for friendly groups.

Part II: Nursery Rhymes My Mother Taught Me

Part II is a rough guide to the tall tales of a number of traditional nursery rhymes. Those chosen for this small volume are emphasized. Original versions of the Part I Parodies are in Part II under the title Nursery Rhymes My Mother Taught Me. The publishers' names are cited along with the earliest known dates of publication. The twenty-four versions as remembered by Giese are those generally found in collections today.

PART I

Nursery Rhymes Your Mother Never Taught You—The Parodies

Food

*for it is good for the heart to be strengthened by grace,
not through foods,
through which those who were so occupied were not benefited.
Hebrews 13:9
(NASB)*

Jack Sprat

Jack Sprat
          would not eat fat,
He thought that he
          would die;

His wife just roared,
          rolled on the floor;
He cried,
          "Cholesterol's high!"

Jack's jolly mate
          the suet ate,
And though her life was
          harried;

She gave him lean
          for his cuisine
And wished she'd never
          married.

Little Ms. Muffet

Little Ms. Muffet
    enjoyed Jimmy Buffet
While eating her curds
    and whey;
The outdoors her diner
    soft grass her recliner
She posed Romanesque
    in her ease.

Now, this lass was a Scrooge,
    never wasted a drop
Of her porridge
    not even a noodle;
Then a Geek spied her spot
    and he liked it a lot
So he offered her fresh
    apple strudel.

Poor Ms. Muffet she fled with her
    hands overhead,
Lost her meal, the whole
    kit and caboodle.
The Nerd watched her go,
    thought her progress was slow,
But he never got up
    to pursue her.

It's hard to foresee
    what the story would be

Had the shy girl complied,
        stayed and ate by his side;
But he was quite content
        with the way that things went,
Sat and drank his cold beer, watched the sun disappear,
        on the tuffet so dear to Ms. Muffet.

Rub-A-Dub-Dub

A butcher, a baker, a candlestick maker,
    went over the hill to see,
A field of wheat, a fatted calf,
    the honey-making bee;

Then 'slash' the grain, 'zip' the throat,
    'squeeze' the waxy hive,
Tomorrow's banquet will be served
    where city people thrive.

Rare roasted beef and buttered loaves,
    will rest on porcelain fine,
With silver spoons reflecting light
    where candelabra shine;

Before dusk falls, the jolly three will jet
    across the sea,
And fetch prime grapes all finely stomped
    for wine from Italy.

RUB-A-DUB-DUB

Peter, Peter

Peter, Peter,
        pizza eater,
Had a wife but
        couldn't please her;

Took her out
        to Taco Bell
And then the marriage
        went quite well.

LITTLE BOY BLUE

Little Boy Blue

Little Boy Blue,
        why do you sleep?
Cows wander at will,
        and so do the sheep.

Sweet clover lures lambs,
        with a scent delicious;
Bugler boy, you must be
        more officious.

The cattle chew boldly,
        for corn stalks appeal,
They chomp yellow cobs
        with unfettered zeal.

    Blow your horn, bugle boy,
        get out of the sack,
    Send the ramblers home
        or they'll never go back.

Reading Between The Lines—Food

Food

1. JACK SPRAT
   What is your philosophy when it comes to food choices?
   How do you feel when others are watching what you eat?
   Are you an all-day eater or a three meals a day person?

2. LITTLE MS. MUFFET
   What friendly gestures of a stranger make you feel uncomfortable?
   What would prompt you to approach someone you don't know?
   Has the internet led you to think differently about strangers? If so how?

3. RUB-A-DUB-DUB
   How much time do you spend thinking about how food gets to your table?
   What label affects your food choices most, 'country of origin' or 'organic'?
   Have you ever visited a working farm?

4. PETER, PETER
   How do you think cultural differences between mates affect a marriage?
   What is your definition of American food?
   What is your favorite ethnic food?

5. LITTLE BOY BLUE
   New mega dairy industrialists milk cows three times a day by machines and never allow the cows out of confinement nor are their calves allowed to suckle.

   What do you think of Little Boy Blue's laissez-faire attitude regarding the animals?
   When animals become objects, how does that affect the way people treat each other?
   If you've been to a zoo, what animal do you make sure you see?

Fun

Pleasant words are a honeycomb,
sweet to the spirit,
and healthful to the body.
Proverbs 16:24
AAT

Mary Had A Little Car

Mary had a little car,
        it's sunroof was her pride,
She drove it to the mall one day
        and offered me a ride.

The boys all looked as we went by,
        the MG doing eighty,
We laughed and waved 'til cops appeared
        and said, "Pull over, lady!"

Pussy Cat, Pussy Cat

"Pussy Cat, Pussy Cat,
    where have you been?"
"I've been to London
    to visit the Queen."

"Pussy Cat, Pussy Cat,
    what did you see?"
"A blue, horse-drawn carriage
    with her Majesty."

"Pussy Cat, dear, did the
    Queen wear a crown?"
"Yes, ermine with diamonds
    and pearls all around."

"Oh, brave Pussy Cat,
    did you watch her sit down?"
"Beneath her Throne was a space
    that I found."

"Pussy Cat, tell, when she spoke
    did you weep?
"I settled quite calmly
    close by her feet."

Pussy Cat, Pussy Cat,
    who spied you there?
"A panicky page
    who was guarding her chair."

> "Pussy Cat, Pussy Cat, what then
> ensued?"
> "He fainted and I thought,
> 'I'd better ski-do'"

June 4, 2014 Viscount Aithrie, a 12 year old page, collapsed 12 feet from Queen Elizabeth II in the House of Lords as the Queen was giving a speech to the assembly.

Pussy Cat, Pussy Cat

Jack And Jill

Jack and Jill
        raced up the hill
to see who could
        run faster.

Jack fell down,
        the crazy clown,
Jill doubled up
        with laughter.

Hickory Dickory Dock

Hickory, Dickory, Dock,
        on drones the schoolroom clock,
At stroke of 'three'
        wild kids run free,
Hickory, Dickory, Dock.

Little Mama Beau-Peep

Little Mama Beau-Peep
   has wandering sheep,
She never knows where
   to find them;

Now they all have I-phones,
   she rings when they roam,
Drives them nuts 'til they're
   home beside her.

Mary, Mary, Quite Contrary

"Mary, Mary, why do you tarry?
    See how your garden grows?
With weeds, not nectar for the bees,
    we need their honey so."

"That silly plot is just a spot
    for flying things that sting me,
And worms that squirm once sod is turned,
    the sight of them is creepy.

"On this stone walk where fairies talk
    I've castles for my dollies;
Where they can dance and dream all day
    of dangerous dolly follies.

"This is MY world and though you think of me
    as quite contrary,
I'll take my ease...do as I please...
    and then a prince I'll marry!"

Reading Between The Lines—Fun

Fun

6. MARY HAD A LITTLE CAR
　　Having a car at 16 is the dream of many teens. At what age did you start driving?
　　How would you feel about being in a car driven by a robotic chauffer?
　　At what age do you think people are the best drivers?

7. PUSSY CAT, PUSSY CAT
　　The story of the 12-year-old page who collapsed twelve feet from Queen Elizabeth as she gave a speech at the House of Lords on June 4, 2014 made national news. The author couldn't resist adding Pussy Cat, Pussy Cat to the story.

　　How interested are you in events that occur among the British Royal family?
　　How do you think Great Britain will fare after Queen Elizabeth dies?
　　What do you think is the great attraction of Downtown Abbey?

8. JACK AND JILL
　　What do you do differently when your opponent is of the opposite sex?
　　What affect will a change of sexual identity have on sports competitions?
　　Competition between men and women can seem friendly, but is it?

9. HICKORY, DICKORY DOCK
　　The United States is tops in spending worldwide on education, but other countries outperform the U. S. in areas of science and math.

Computers are in student's backpacks instead of books. What do you think of that?
"Drone" has a new meaning today. What are your thoughts about drones?
Who was your favorite teacher?

10. LITTLE MAMA BEAU-PEEP

At what age is a child old enough to handle an iPhone?
What consequences do you see if land phones become obsolete?
How do you protect yourself from identity theft?

11. MARY, MARY, QUITE CONTRARY

Do you think contrary persons are egotists or independent thinkers and doers?
When does a child start thinking of others as well as him/her self?
How can children be prepared for the realities of life without destroying their dreams?

People

The eyes of the Lord are in every place,
Watching the evil and the good.
Proverbs 15:3
(NASB)

There Was An Old Woman

There was an old woman
        who lived on the shore,
She wanted no husband
        just children galore.

She went to the sperm bank
        a donor to choose,
Young, tall, and handsome who
        wore blue suede shoes.

Her trips were successful,
        and joy did abound 'til
much later a flock of step-siblings
        were found.

They bonded together and
        searched for their dad,
For DNA linked them—both
        good and the bad.

In an old trailer home
        they discovered their match,
A hippie who lived a vague
        vagabond past.

The man who could claim them
        fell back in surprise,

Twirled his pony tail, cried out,
"My nose and my eyes!"

September 6, 2011. The New York Times, New York Edition Headline; p.D1: From One Sperm Donor, 150 Children.

Georgie Porgy

Georgie Porgy had an eye
For winsome girls who walked on by

His bold approach worked on them quick
Wore fancy clothes and acted slick

He offered them a cold Mai-Tai
Then puckered up and made them cry

The boys came out and gave him chase
But Georgie ran and hid his face

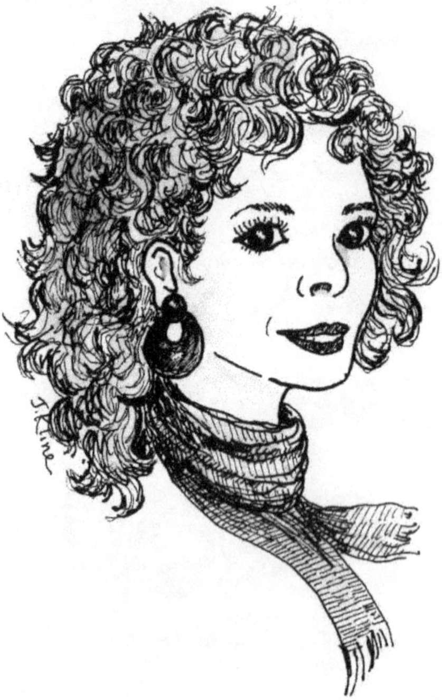

Three Blind Mice

Three blind mice, three blind mice,
Cowards thrice, cowards thrice,

They ran after skirts like the farmer's wife,
She wised up and sharpened her carving knife,

The lawyers arrived just to save the lives
Of three blind mice.

Baa, Baa, Black Sheep

"Baa, Baa, Black Sheep,
Have you any stuff?"
"Yes sir, yes sir, never enough.

"Some for the head man
who walks with a cane,
and bags for young runners who sell in the lane.

A Diller, A Dollar

A diller, a dollar,
          why do you bother
A scholar's robe to take?

You think you're smart,
          roam through the park,
Smooch with girls after dark.

You sleep till noon,
          lie in your room
And dream that you are spooning;

You'll soon be poor
          no job secure
For acting like a loony

Little Jack Horner

Little Jack Horner
        went to the corner,
Looking for holiday pie,

He carried a gun, searched
        the streets for a plum,
He desperately wanted a high.

Snow scrunched under his foot
        on a path he didn't know,
To his ears came a sweet, mellow sound;

Church bells chimed all around,
        on the curb he sat down,
In his coat he came up with a weed.

The joint was a joke
        but he inhaled the smoke
And his mother was pleased as could be.

From her heart came a sigh,
        she looked Jack in the eye,
Put a log on the fire, poured hot tea;

Jack smiled at her joy,
        spun her round like a toy,
All aglow as a bright Christmas tree;

Though it could be a lie,
        the young maverick did cry,
"Mama dear, what a good boy am I."

LITTLE JACK HORNER

Reading Between
The Lines—People

PEOPLE

12. THERE WAS AN OLD WOMAN
In 1952 the first donated sperm were used to impregnate three woman whose partners could not produce viable sperm. On September 6, 2011 The New York Times reported that one donor was responsible for the birth of 150 children.

If DNA tests protected against marrying a close relative, in this day of internet romances, what would you think of requiring the test?
Were you first, middle or last child in your family? Which do you wish you were?
Population control was a hot topic in the 1960's. How did the preaching affect you?

13. GEORGIE PORGY
In the 1960's my daughters were warned to drink only capped drinks at parties as LSD was being sneaked into women's drinks as a joke. In the 2000's drugs in drinks have been used to prevent the naïve from resisting unwanted sexual advances.

At what age were you introduced to alcoholic drinks?
How does the #ME Too movement affect you?
What can be done to create respect between men and women?

14. THREE BLIND MICE
In 1993 Lorena Bobbitt stopped her husband's unwanted advances with a carving knife!

Do you think Lorena Bobbitt was inspired by the Three Blind Mice nursery rhyme?
Which U.S. Presidents with sexual appetites might be likened to the three blind mice?

How much freedom did you have from your parents' oversight after the age of 12?

15. BAA, BAA, BLACK SHEEP

When I was young, those who got in trouble were considered the 'black sheep' of the family. It had nothing to do with skin color. The wool of black sheep was out of favor in the 1700's and earlier because it could not be dyed.

Do you carry your groceries in a bag or a sack?
If you had a small special bag as a child, what did you keep in it?
Were you ever considered the 'black sheep' of your family? If so, why?

16. A DILLAR A DOLLAR

How many times did you switch primary schools? High schools?
In the '80's' inclusion was for kids who had learning disabilities. What does 'inclusion' mean today in your town?
Who was the bully in your school?

17. LITTLE JACK HORNER

Why does Little Jack Horner think he is a good boy?
How does music affect your mood?
How concerned are you about the effects of legalizing marijuana?

Politics

*But let justice roll down like waters
And righteousness like an ever-flowing stream.
Amos 5:24
(NASB)*

All Around

All around the
        Covenant tree
The Muslim raced
        the Hebrew,
The Christian tried to judge
        the outcome,
"Cease" cried the Holy
        One.

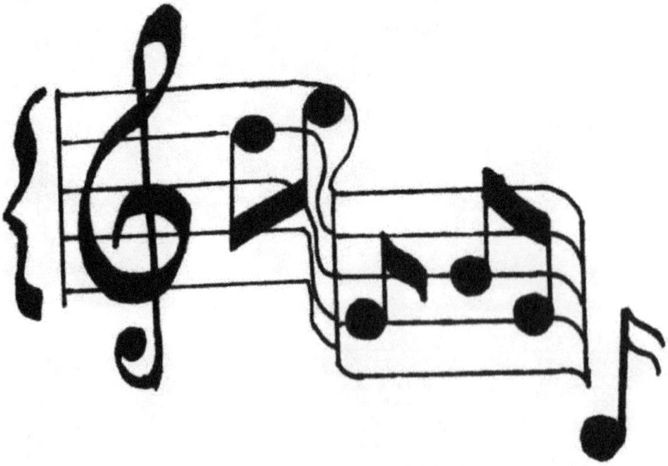

Old (Nat) King Cole

Old King Cole
        had a musical soul,
And a musical soul had he;

His lyrical voice,
        spinning tunes of his choice,
Brought fame to his trio of three.

The King, and the Duke,
        Ellington by name, played rich music
That brought each man royal acclaim.

Mellow song filled the air,
        trusty fans loved their flair,
Cheered their gigs in the land of the free.

Unforgettable reigns,
        still tradition restrained
Dukes and Kings who sought lodging to gain.

Doors were closed every night
        to those NOT colored white,
"No room" was the well-worn refrain.

Humpty Dumpty

Humpty Dumpty
        needed a wall
You could not jump
        over
Or under it
        crawl.

He'd sit on the
        top
With his spy glass
        in hand,
Watch over his fiefdom,
        an ideal land.

Oh, he'd bluster if south winds
        sent sand up his snout;
Then he'd totter a little,
        and claim he did not;

And, the sound of kids wailing
        outside his high perch
Would do nothing to stop armed
        patrols in their search.

Still Humpty is praying
        he'll rise with his wall;
Though his shell is quite fragile,
        he hopes not to fall,

For folks who oppose him
 would watch him come down
And snatch his gold crown
 as it dropped to the ground.

Hey Diddle Diddle

Hey diddle diddle
        crazed scientists fiddle
With nature's inviolate
        rules,
While copycats giggle,
        build clones that will wiggle,
John Q wants to stop
        at the moon.

Simple Simon

Simple Simon met a frat man
        on his way to college,
Said Simon to the Greek guy,
        "I'm going to get knowledge."

Said the vain chap who saw the lad
        wore clothing that was crummy,
"Do you not know to graduate
        you'll need a lot of money?"

"A student loan can be my own, I'll pay back
        what they ask me."
"You naïve one, usury fees
        will bleed you till you're on your knees."

The North Wind Doth Blow

The North wind doth blow
  and we shall have snow
And what will the homeless do then,
  poor things;

They'll sleep in a spot
  with a blanket, no cot,
And hope for some food that is hot,
  poor things.

They'll sleep in a spot
  with a blanket, no cot,
And hope for some food
  that is hot.

WHO KILLED COCK ROBIN

Who Killed Cock Robin?

"Who killed Cock Robin?"
"I" said the hunter,
"With my trusty bow and arrow,
I killed Cock Robin."

"Who saw him die?"
"I" said the sky,
"With my blue, naked eye,
I saw him die."

"Who will make his shroud?"
"I" said the naturalist,
"With details I am serious.
"I'll make his shroud."

"Who caught his blood?"
"I" said the bacteriologist,
"In my glass petri dish.
I caught his blood."

"Who will carry the torch?"
"I" said the environmentalist,
"I'll call up my list.
I'll carry the torch."

"Who will be the clerk?"
"I" said the statistician,
"I'll record his condition.
I'll be the clerk."

"Who will dig his grave?"
      "I" said the wealthy contractor,
"And build upon it soon after.
      I'll dig his grave."

"Who will be the parson?"
      "I" said the tall Evangelist,
"His good deed I'll recall.
      I'll be the parson."

"Who will be chief mourner?"
      "I" said the teary-eyed child
without a smile,
      "I'll be the chief mourner."

"Who will sing a psalm?"
      "I" said a sweet lady
going on eighty,
      "I'll sing a psalm."

"Who will carry the coffin?"
      "I" said the gardener,
Whose chemicals harmed him,
      "I'll carry the coffin."

"Who will toll the bell?"
      "I" said the lobbyist,
My power no one will resist,
      I'll not desist."

All the birds of the air,
      chirped a dirge of despair
When they heard the death knell
      for Cock Robin.

Reading Between The Lines—Politics

POLITICS

18. ALL AROUND
Jews, Muslims and Christians all claim Abraham and the covenant God made with Abraham, in the Biblical book Genesis, as a trademark of their faith, although in varying degrees.

What contrasting communities of faith are in your city?
With what areas of Artificial Intelligence are you comfortable?
What do you see as the effect of self-directed faith on today's youngest generation?

19. OLD (NAT) ING COLE
When the Civil Rights Act of 1964 was passed, equality for African Americans began, although it did not do away with all discrimination.

If you saw the movie _Green Book_, what surprised you?
Where do you see discrimination today among those you know?
What is it about music that links people of all races, creeds and colors?

20. HUMPTY DUMPTY
How has the influx of undocumented immigrants affected your life?
Have you ever actively campaigned for a political candidate?
What would cause the White Supremacists' and the Aryan Nation to fail?

21. HEY DIDDLE DIDDLE
The rhyme about the cow jumping over the moon seemed outlandish until 1969 when Neil Armstrong stepped on the moon's surface.

What is your favorite science fiction book or movie?
How long do you wait before trying some new-fangled gadget?
What is your opinion of space exploration?

22. SIMPLE SIMON
In 2019, the average student loan debt for 1 out of 10 householders age 50 and over was $33,000. Federal loan penalties for defaulting can include taking a portion of tax refund, withholding a percent of

Social Security retirement or disability benefits, and garnishing some of the borrower's wages. (AARP Bulletin/Real Possibilities July/August 2019).

    Would you rather have a new car or a college degree?
    What is the benefit of a trade union? Plumber, painter, electrician, teacher?
    How would you chose a University today: for location, majors offered, a party school, or one with a high rating academically or sports wise?

23. THE NORTH WIND

    In the financial crash of 2008 thousands lost their homes. Homelessness drives foster care placements.

    Have you ever been or do you know someone who has been homeless?
    Where are the homeless shelters in your area?
    If you have gone camping, was it with tents or an RV?

24. WHO KILLED COCK ROBIN

    What is your favorite outdoor recreation?
    Are you a member of any group organized to protect the environment?
    How many culprits do you see in this new version of Who Killed Cock Robin?

PART II

Traditional Nursery Rhymes
My Mother Taught Me

About The History Of Traditional Nursery Rhymes

Nursery rhymes were rarely designed for children. They have moved through the centuries with rumors of hidden meanings and changing implications as the times dictate. They are often enigmatic and continue to be the topic of much conjecture.

The origin of Jack and Jill can find a connection to Scandinavia, however, the first publication of the version we know today was published in 1795. That was two years after King Louis XVI of France and his wife Marie Antoinette were beheaded as part of the 1793 Reign of Terror in France. Some have suggested Jack and Jill refer to Louie and Marie as their heads rolled off the executioner's block.

Georgie Porgie is another rhyme connected with France, although the villain is an Englishman, George Villiers, the First Duke of Buckingham. (1592-1628). Villiers had an affair with Anne of Austria, the wife of King Louis XIII of France. King James I of England kept George out of trouble for a while because of his own undercover relationship with Villiers.

Little Jack Horner is popularly connected to the dissolutions of monasteries in England by King Henry VIII after he broke away from the Catholic church (1534). Stories grew about a steward named Horner and how he gained ownership of some of the land confiscated from the Roman Catholic Church. Horner's ancestors deny the charge to this day.

Oral versions of nursery rhymes circulated throughout Northern Europe for generations before they were put on paper. Most were first published in the late 18th and early 19th centuries in England. The Oxford Dictionary of Nursery Rhymes (Oxford University Press, 1997) lists 800 rhymes with publishing dates and anecdotes of their origin. This specialized dictionary is full of many interesting historical details.

Although nursery rhymes, in general, are often called Mother Goose rhymes, the first book published (1697) in which the name "Mother Goose" was used contained eight tales but no rhymes. Among the stories were Sleeping Beauty, Cinderella, and Puss in Boots. A Frenchman, Charles Perrault, collected and published them, but he did not invent them. He called the collection Mere l'Oye— Mother Goose. In 1729 John Newberry put out a tiny, illustrated book for children called Mother Goose's Melody. It contained 52 rhymes and 15 songs from Shakespeare's plays. Newberry was the first to associate rhymes as well as stories with Mother Goose.

About Traditional Nursery Rhymes Today

Attempts have been made since 1641 to "suppress or alter" some traditional nursery rhymes. Many "are alleged to arouse sadistic tendencies" in children. (Oxford Dictionary of Verses, footnote, p.2) In the Victorian Age the British 'Society for Nursery Rhyme Reform' was formed. As late as 1941, the Society condemned 100 common nursery rhymes for "harbouring unsavory elements." Max Minckler (Riffle Poetry)

Sean Braswell, in The Daily Dose, January 27, 2017 writes, "It's time to kill off Mother Goose." Braswell is the father of several young daughters. He is appalled by the lowly picture of a female's character and place in society that is painted by many traditional nursery rhymes. It is not the image he wants his girls to have of themselves as women.

Bruno Bettelheim (1903—1990) criticized revisionism. He argued that revised versions of nursery rhymes may not perform the functions of catharsis for children that allow them to deal with violence and danger in an imaginative way. Bettelheim's educational background in psychology and psychiatry is murky at best. (Wikipedia.) Some of Bettelheim's students at the Orthogenic School of the University of Chicago claim he was abusive to them. Bettelheim followed Freud's view that neurotic children were the result of 'frozen mothers.'

In the late 20th century revisionism became associated with 'political correctness.' Instead of new rhymes, variations on the ones learned in childhood are reworked to fit new circumstances. Some are just for fun: Anthology of Comical Rhymes, Bruce Lansky, ©2006, Meadowbrook Press. Some teach social responsibility: The Green Mother Goose, Jan Peck and David Davis, ©2011, Sterling Publishing Co., Inc. Some are learning tools for the very young: Barney's Favorite Mother Goose Rhymes, Published by Barney Publishing™, division of The Lyons Group™, ©1993.

Revisions of nursery rhymes are likewise used in advertising various products. In the past century, William Wrigley had "14,000,000 'Mother Goose' books rewritten to tie chewing-gum into nursery jingles" (Oxford Dictionary of Rhymes, p.40.) In the 2000's there is a trend in television ads to reference lines from popular nursery rhymes. In 2019, an ad had a father playing 'I'm a little tea pot' with his young daughter. Crossword puzzles also use clues from nursery rhymes to discover words.

Nursery rhymes that are set to music are purchased to soothe the younger child. They are more in the line of lullabies and provide a pleasant background at naptime. According to the Chicago Tribune, August 14, 1994 (AP) "Research supports the assertion that music and rhyme increase a child's ability in spatial reasoning, which aids math skills."

Occupying ourselves with nursery rhymes does not seem to lose its fascination. In 2014, Seth Lerer, Dean of Arts and Humanity at the University of California—San Diego, spoke on <u>NBC's Today show</u>. He said, "Nursery Rhymes are a triumph of the power of oral history...When we sing (rhymes) we're participating in something that bonds parent and child." (BBC Britain.)

Traditional Nursery Rhymes

Nursery Rhymes My Mother Taught Me—Food

First Publication Dates

JACK SPRAT   *John Ray—1670; Mother Goose's Melodies—1765*
    Jack Sprat could not eat fat
        his wife could eat not lean
    And so between the two of them
        they licked the platter clean.

LITTLE MISS MUFFET   *Songs for the Nursery—1805*
    Little Miss Muffet sat on a tuffet
        eating her curds and whey,
    Along came a spider and sat down beside her
        and frightened Miss Muffet away.

RUB-A-DUB-DUB   *Christmas Box, vol. ii;—1798*
    Rub-a-dub-dub, three men in a tub
        all went out to sea,
    A butcher, a baker, a candlestick maker
        singing merrily.

PETER, PETER   *Infant Institutes—1797; Mother Goose's Quarto—1825*
    Peter, Peter, pumpkin eater
        had a wife and couldn't keep her,
    Put her in a pumpkin shell
        and there he kept her very well.

LITTLE BOY BLUE   <u>Famous Tom Thumb...1760,; (three voices glee,) Infant Institutes—1797</u>
Little boy blue, come blow your horn,
    the sheep's in the meadow, the cow's in the corn,
Oh where is the boy that looks after the sheep?
    He's under a haystack fast asleep.

Nursey Rhymes My Mother Taught Me—Fun

First Publication Date

MARY HAD A LITTLE LAMB *Poems for Our Children; Mrs. Sarah J. Hale—1830*

Mary had a little lamb,*
it's fleece was white as snow
And everywhere that Mary went
the lamb was sure to go.
It followed her to school one day
which was against the rule,
It made the children laugh and play
to see a lamb at school.

* *Mary had a little lamb*, was the first utterance Thomas Edison recorded on his new talking machine, the phonograph, in 1877. The poem was written by the American Sarah J. Hale in Boston, Massachusetts in 1830.

PUSSY CAT, PUSSY CAT *Songs for the Nursery—1805*

Pussy Cat, Pussy Cat, where have you been?
I've been to London to visit the Queen.
Pussy Cat, Pussy Cat, what did you there?
I frightened a little mouse under her chair.

JACK AND JILL *(origin traced to Norse myth) Mother Goose's Melody—1765*

Jack and Jill went up the hill
to fetch a pail of water,
Jack fell down and broke his crown,
and Jill came tumbling after.

HICKORY DICKORY DOCK *Tom Thumb's Pretty Song Book——1744*

    Hickory, Dickory, Dock, the mouse ran up the clock,
        the clock struck one,
the mouse ran down,
        Hickory, Dickory, Dock.

LITTLE BO-PEEP *Francis Douce MS, Critical Comments on the Bo-peepeid—1805*

    Little Bo-Peep has lost her sheep
        and can't tell where to find them.
    Leave them alone, and they'll come home,
        wagging their tails behind them.

MARY, MARY, QUITE CONTRARY *Tom Thumb's Pretty Song Book——1744*

    Mary, Mary, quite contrary, how does your garden grow?
    With silver bells and cockleshells and pretty maids all in a row.

Nursey Rhymes My Mother Taught Me—People

First Publication Date

THE WOMAN WHO LIVED IN A SHOE   *Gammer Gurton's Garland*—1784
  There was an old woman who lived in a shoe,
    she had so many children she didn't know what to do,
  She gave them some broth without any bread,
    and whipped them all soundly and put them to bed.

GEORGIE PORGY   *James Orchard Halliwell, The Nursery Rhymes of England*—1842
  Georgie Porgie, puddin', pie,
    kissed the girls and made them cry.
  When the boys came out to play,
    Georgie Porgie ran away.

THREE BLIND MICE   *Deuteromelia, Thomas Ravenscroft*—1609
  Three blind mice, three blind mice,
    see how they run, see how they run.
  They all ran after the farmer's wife,
    she cut off their tails with a carving knife,
  Did ever you see such a sight in your life,
    as three blind mice.

BAA BAA BLACK SHEEP *Tom Thumbs Pretty Song Book (M. Cooper), vol.ii;*—1744
  Baa Baa Black Sheep, have you any wool?
    Yes Sir! Yes, Sir! Three bags full.
  One for my Master and one for his Dame
    And one for the little boy who lives in the lane.

A DILLER A DOLLAR — *Gammer Gurton's Garland—1784*

A diller, a dollar, a ten o'clock scholar,
    what makes you come so soon?
You used to come at ten o'clock,
    but now you come at noon.

LITTLE JACK HORNER — *Namby Pamby, Henry Carey—1725 (1726)*

Little Jack Horner sat in a corner
    eating his Christmas pie,
He put in his thumb and pulled out a plumb,
    and said what a good boy am I.

Nursery Rhymes My Mother Taught Me—Politics

<u>*First Publication Date*</u>

POP GOES THE WEASEL*   1855
    All around the mulberry bush, the monkey chased the weasel,
        the monkey thought was all in fun,
    Pop! goes the weasel!

    **Pop Goes the Weasel is not included in The Oxford Dictionary of Nursery Rhymes, but it is in The Secret History of Nursery Rhymes by Linda Alchin, where two versions of lyrics are recorded. The above is how I remember the childhood version I learned. A completely different The Mulberry Bush rhyme starts "Here we go round the mulberry bush." Though popular in the U.S.A, it, also, is not included in The Oxford Dictionary of Nursery Rhymes.*

HEY DIDDLE DIDDLE   <u>*Mother Goose's Melody—c.1765*</u>
    Hey diddle, diddle, the cat and the fiddle,
        the cow jumped over the moon.
    The little dog laughed to see such sport,
        and the dish ran away with the spoon.

HUMPTY DUMPTY   <u>*Juvenile Amusements—1797*</u>
    Humpty Dumpty sat on a wall
        Humpty Dumpty had a great fall,
    All the king's horses and all the king's men
        couldn't put Humpty together again.

OLE KING COLE
Useful Transactions in Philosophy, William King, 1708—9

Ole King Cole was a merry old soul,
    and a merry old soul was he.
He called for his pipe, and he called for his bowl,
    and he called for his fiddlers three.

SIMPLE SIMON
Simple Simon, chapbook advertised by C. Dicey and R. Marshall—1764

Simple Simon met a pie man going to the fair.
Said Simple Simon to the pie man, "Let me taste your ware."
Said the pie man to Simple Simon, "Give me first your penny"
Said Simple Simon to the pie man, "Sir, I haven't any".

THE NORTH WIND
Songs for the Nursery—1805

The North wind doth blow,
    and we shall have snow,
And what will poor robin do then.
    poor thing.

WHO KILLED COCK
first four verses only: Tom Thumbs Pretty Song Book c.1744
Entire rhyme after 1788

Who killed Cock Robin?
    I, said the sparrow
        With my bow and arrow,
I killed Cock Robin

Who saw him die?
    I, said the fly,
        With my little eye,
I saw him die.

Who caught his blood?
    I, said the fish,
        With my little dish,
I caught his blood.

Who'll make his shroud?
    I, said the beetle,
        With my thread and needle,
I'll make the shroud.

Who'll dig his grave?
    I, said the owl,
        With my pick and shovel,
I'll dig his grave.

Who'll be the parson?
    I, said the rook,
        With my little book,
I'll be the parson.

Who'll be the clerk?
    I, said the lark,
        If it's not in the dark,
I'll be the clerk.

Who'll carry the link? (torch)
    I, said the linnet,
        I'll fetch it in a minute
I'll carry the link.

Who'll be chief mourner?
    I, said the dove,
        I mourn for my love,
I'll be chief mourner.

Who'll carry the coffin?
    I, said the kite,
        If it's not through the night,
I'll carry the coffin.

Who'll sing a psalm?
    I, said the thrush,
        As she sat on a bush,
I'll sing a psalm.

Who'll toll the bell?
    I, said the bull,
        Because I can pull,
I'll toll the bell.

All the birds of the air
    went a-sighing and a-sobbing,
        When they heard the bell tolling
For poor Cock Robin.

The Oxford Dictionary of Nursery Rhymes notes that a fifteenth-century stained glass window at Buckland Rectory, Gloucester, England, shows a bird with the markings of a robin pierced through the heart with an arrow.

Acknowledgments And After Thoughts

Until I started putting together Nursery Rhymes Your Mother Never Taught You, I had no idea how pervasive the originals are in our everyday world. The Oxford Dictionary of Nursery Rhymes states that in 1997 someone counted 35 editions of nursery rhymes available in one Chicago bookstore.

My search for information started with The World Book Encyclopedia. Two sections, <u>Nursery Rhymes,</u> and <u>Mother Goose,</u> had similar but somewhat different material. Next I opened Wikipedia. The site had good information, and, some references that brought me to the library. I was able to check out The Oxford Dictionary of Nursery Rhymes, a volume containing over 500 rhymes and songs with historical notes on all and many interesting sidebars. The other useful book I wanted was hard to find. The West Aurora library research librarian searched and obtained from the Ames, Iowa library a charming, colorful book called The Secret History of Nursery Rhymes. The author is Linda Alchin, a British citizen. The small book has illustrations for each rhyme and tales Alchin chose to go along with them. The simplicity of the book does not take away from its value as far as probing different perspectives on the history of the included rhymes.

Last of all, I went to Google with 'nursery rhymes' as my search. There are more sites than I wanted to pursue, but the ones I found assured me that people are still putting their "two-cents worth" in where nursery rhymes are concerned.

Because much information was duplicated in all of the published sources, it was hard to attach one source to most of the content of Nursery Rhymes Your Mother Never Taught You. When it seemed useful and possible, I did so. The <u>Selected References</u> contain pertinent information on resources used.

I want to thank my family and friends and the Illinois State Poetry Society for listening to my silly ditties over the past few years. They encouraged me to publish my parodies. Their support put me on a very interesting journey into a world still vibrating with energy.

"A merry heart doeth good like a medicine."
May it be so for you.
Marilyn Huntman Giese
October 4, 2019

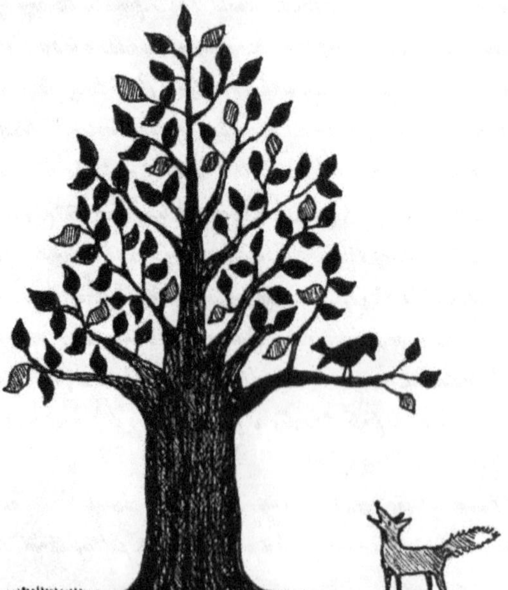
J. Kline

Selected References

Dictionaries and Encyclopedias

    Opie, Iona and Peter, Ed. *The Oxford Dictionary of Nursery Rhymes*, New Edition. Oxford, New York: Oxford University Press, 1997.

    The World Book Encyclopedia, vol. M and N. Field Enterprises Educational Corporation. Copyright 1963, U.S.A.

History

    Alchin, Linda. *The Secret History of Nursery Rhymes*. Imprint: Mitcham, England: Neilsen, 2013. Copyright Linda Alchin, 2013.

Additional Source

    Wikipedia/Nursery Rhymes

Author's Favorite Children's Nursery Rhyme Book

    Kelly, Miles. *Illustrated Treasury of Nursery Rhymes*. Miles Kelly Publishing Ltd. 2014, Harding's Barn, Bardfield End Green, Thaxted, Essex, CM6 3PX, UK. 2017. Printed in China.

    Cover Photo
    The ancient Roman wall at L'Antic Bocoi del Gotic, Barcelona, Spain